GREAT ILLUSTRATED CLASSICS

AESOP'S FABLES

BARONET BOOKS, New York, New York

GREAT ILLUSTRATED CLASSICS

edited by
Rochelle Larkin

ABOUT · THE · AUTHOR

Aesop is thought to have lived from the end of the sixth to the seventh centuries B.C. He was a slave whose skill in telling stories led to his being freed by one of his masters. Aesop's stories were so loved that he was welcomed to tell them even at the courts of kings.

Although Aesop lived in ancient Greece, his stories may have come from other countries, as well as earlier times. What is certain is that people all over the world have collected and enjoyed these tales for thousands of years.

In these stories, animals speak with humans as well as with each other. They are always in interesting situations that need cleverness and understanding to solve the problems, real or imagined, that occur. It was part of Aesop's great skill to give human characteristics to animals and make them believable, and at the same time tell us of ways to deal with whatever faces us in life.

Quotations from *Aesop's Fables* have become part of our language. And sometimes the stories are even funny!

Passing and Overtaking the Sleeping Hare

The · Tortoise · and · the · Hare

A Hare mocked a Tortoise for his slow manner. The Tortoise promptly challenged her to a race. The Hare quickly agreed.

They began and soon the Hare left the Tortoise way behind. Midway through the race she became bored and began to snack on some leafy grass. The noon day sun was glaring in the sky and the Hare grew quite warm. Seeing she was far ahead, she found a shady spot and went to sleep, knowing she could always catch the Tortoise. Meanwhile he plugged along in his slow way, passing and then overtaking the sleeping Hare.

The Hare, having overslept, awoke from her nap and realized the Tortoise had passed her by. She took off at full speed, but run as fast as she would, she could not catch up. The Tortoise reached the finish line first and won.

✳

Slow and steady wins the race.

THE · FOX · AND · THE · GRAPES

A hungry Fox saw some fine bunches of Grapes hanging from a vine that was trained along a high trellis, and did his best to reach them by jumping as high as he could into the air.

But it was all in vain, for they were just out of reach: so he gave up trying, and walked away with an air of dignity and unconcern, remarking, "I thought those Grapes were ripe, but I see now they are quite sour."

✳

Small-minded people scorn what they can't have.

They Were Just Out of Reach.

THE · WOLF · IN · SHEEP'S · CLOTHING

A Wolf once found a Sheep's skin, and, thinking he would have an easy way of getting his prey, wrapped himself in it and slipped into the sheepfold with the flock, intending to kill all he wanted during the night.

But soon after the Shepherd had made the door fast, he found he had nothing for supper, and, going in with an ax to kill a sheep, he mistook the Wolf for one of them and killed him on the spot.

✳

The wicked often fall into their own traps.

He Wrapped Himself in It.

THE · BOY · WHO · CRIED · WOLF

A shepherd's Boy was tending his flock near a village, and thought it would be great fun to hoax the villagers by pretending that a Wolf was attacking the sheep: so he shouted out, "Wolf! Wolf!" and when the people came running up, he laughed at them for their pains.

He did this more than once, and every time the villagers found they had been hoaxed, for there was no Wolf at all.

At last a Wolf really did come, and the Boy cried, "Wolf! Wolf!" as loud as he could: but the people were so used to hearing him call that they took no notice of his cries for help. And so the Wolf had it all his own way, and killed off sheep after sheep at his pleasure.

✳

You cannot believe a liar even when he tells the truth.

He Shouted "Wolf! Wolf!"

THE · GRASSHOPPER · AND · THE · ANTS

One fine day in winter some Ants were busy drying their store of corn, which had gotten rather damp during a long spell of rain.

Presently a Grasshopper came up and begged them to spare her a few grains. "For," she said, "I'm simply starving."

The Ants stopped work for a moment, though this was against their principles. "May we ask," said they, "what you were doing with yourself all last summer? Why didn't you collect a store of food for the winter?"

"The fact is," replied the Grasshopper, "I was so busy singing that I hadn't the time."

"If you spent the summer singing," replied the Ants, "you can't do better than to spend the winter dancing." And they chuckled and went on with their work.

✳

Never lose a good opportunity.

The Ants Stopped Work for a Moment.

THE · FOX · AND · THE · LION

*T*he first time a Fox saw a Lion he was so terrified that he almost died of fright.

When he saw him again, he was still afraid, but hid his fear.

But when he met him the third time, he was so brave he began to talk to him as though they were old friends.

✳

Familiarity breeds contempt.

He Almost Died of Fright.

THE · TWO · POTS

*T*wo Pots, one made of clay and the other brass, were carried together on the tide. The Brass Pot told the Clay that if she stayed close to him, he would be sure to protect her.

"Thank you," said the other, "but that is just what I will not do. If you are at a distance, I may float in safety, but should we come together I am sure to be the worse for it."

✳

Too-powerful neighbors should be avoided,
for in a quarrel, the weaker suffers.

He Would be Sure to Protect Her.

THE · FOX · AND · THE · STORK

A Fox invited a Stork to dinner, at which the only food he provided was a large flat dish of soup. The Fox lapped it up with great relish, but the Stork with her long bill tried in vain to eat the tasty broth.

Her distress caused the sly Fox much amusement. But not long after, the Stork invited him in turn, and set before him a pitcher with a long and narrow neck, into which she could get her bill with ease.

Thus, while she enjoyed her dinner, the Fox sat by hungry and helpless, for it was impossible for him to reach the tempting contents of the vessel.

✳

*Those who play jokes on others
must expect them in return.*

The Stork Tried in Vain.

THE · LEOPARD · AND · THE · THREE · BULLS

A Leopard was watching three Bulls, wanting to seize them for his food.

His chances would be better when the Bulls separated, but they enjoyed being together so much that wherever one was, the others were sure to be as well.

Knowing he must capture them one by one, if at all, the Leopard began to spread rumors among the Bulls until he had created so much jealousy and distrust among them, that they moved away from each other.

When the Leopard saw that they had separated from one another, he attacked each one, and so made an easy conquest of them all.

✳

Friends' fights are their enemies' opportunities.

A Leopard was Watching Three Bulls.

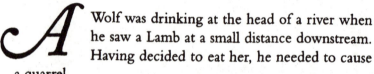

THE · WOLF · AND · THE · LAMB

A Wolf was drinking at the head of a river when he saw a Lamb at a small distance downstream. Having decided to eat her, he needed to cause a quarrel.

"How dare you spoil my water?" he demanded.

"How can I spoil the water, since it goes from you to me, not me to you?" asked the Lamb.

"Never mind that," said the Wolf, "a year ago you called me many bad names!"

"A year ago I was not even born yet!" said the trembling Lamb

"Well," replied the Wolf, "if it wasn't you, it was your father. It's no use trying to talk me out of my supper;" and he grabbed upon the helpless Lamb and ate her.

✳

The tyrant always finds an excuse
to injure the innocent.

"How Dare You Spoil My Water?"

THE · CAT · AND · THE · BIRDS

A Cat heard that the Birds in an aviary were ailing.

So he got himself up as a doctor, and taking with him a set of the instruments proper to that profession, presented himself at the door, and inquired after the health of the Birds.

"We shall do very well," they replied, without letting him in, "when we've seen the last of you!"

✳

A villain in disguise will not deceive the wise.

So He Got Himself Up as a Doctor.

THE · SPENDTHRIFT · AND · THE · SWALLOW

A Spendthrift, who had wasted his fortune, and had nothing left but the clothes in which he stood, saw a Swallow one fine day in early spring.

Thinking that summer had come, and that he could now do without his coat, he went and sold it for what it would fetch.

A change, however, took place in the weather, and there came a sharp frost which killed the unfortunate Swallow. When the Spendthrift saw its body he cried, "Miserable bird! Thanks to you I am perishing of cold myself."

✳

One swallow does not make a whole summer.

He Went and Sold It.

THE · MOON · AND · HER · MOTHER

The Moon once asked her Mother to make her a gown that would fit her well.

"How," replied she, "can I make a gown to fit you when you are first a new Moon, then a full Moon, and then neither one nor the other?"

✳

Changeable people are not easily satisfied.

The Moon Asked Her Mother.

THE · LION ·
AND · THE · MOUSE

A Lion asleep in his lair was waked by a Mouse running over his face. The Lion seized it and was about to kill it.

The Mouse begged for its life. "Please let me go," it cried, "and one day I will repay your kindness."

The idea of so small a creature ever doing anything for him amused the Lion so much that he laughed and let it go.

But the Mouse's chance came, after all. One day the Lion got entangled in a net which had been spread by some hunters; the Mouse recognized his roars and ran to the spot.

It set to work to gnaw the ropes, and succeeded in setting the Lion free. "There!" said the Mouse, "You laughed at me when I promised I would repay you: now you see, even a Mouse can help a Lion!"

✻

No good deed goes unrewarded.

The Lion Seized It with His Paw.

THE · FLIES · AND · THE · HONEY-POT

A swarm of Flies found a Honey-pot which had been upset and would not leave the spot while there was a single drop left.

After a while the honey even stuck to their feet and wings and they could not fly away.

Then they cried, "What stupid creatures we are! For a short hour's pleasure we have thrown away our lives!"

✳

The greedy never know when they have had enough.

The Honey Stuck to Their Feet and Wings.

THE · NORTH · WIND · AND · THE · SUN

The North Wind and the Sun each claimed he was the stronger. At last they agreed to try their powers upon a traveler, to see which could soonest strip him of his cloak.

The North Wind tried first: gathering up all his force, he came whirling furiously down upon the man, and caught up his cloak as though he would take it from him by one single effort. But the harder he blew, the more closely the man wrapped it round himself.

Then the Sun beamed gently on the traveler, who unclasped his cloak and left it hanging loosely about his shoulders: then the Sun shone in full strength, and the man was glad to throw off his cloak and go on his journey more lightly clad.

✳

Persuasion is better than force.

The Harder He Blew

THE · HARES · AND · THE · FROGS

The Hares once gathered to cry about their unhappiness, being exposed to dangers on all sides and lacking strength and courage. Men, dogs, birds and beasts were all their enemies, and killed and devoured them: sooner than endure such persecution, they determined to end their lives.

They rushed to a neighboring pool, intending to drown themselves.

On the bank were a number of Frogs, who, hearing the noise of the Hares, leaped into the water and hid themselves there.

Then one of the older, wiser Hares cried out, "Stop, friends, take heart; don't let us destroy ourselves. For here are creatures who are afraid of us, and who must be still more timid than ourselves."

✳

There are always others worse off than you are.

They Rushed to a Pool.

THE · FOX · AND · THE · GOAT

A Fox fell into a well and was unable to get out. A thirsty Goat came by, and asked him if the water was good.

"Good?" said the Fox. "It's the best I ever tasted! Come try it yourself."

The Goat jumped in at once. When he had enough to drink, he looked for a way to get out.

The Fox said, "I have an idea. Stand on your hind legs, with your forelegs against the side of the well. I'll climb on to your back, and by stepping on your horns, I can get out. When I'm out, I'll help you out, too."

The Goat did so. The Fox climbed on to his back and out of the well; then he coolly walked away.

The Goat loudly reminded him of his promise but the Fox said, "If you had any sense, you wouldn't have got in without seeing that you could get out again."

✳

Look before you leap.

The Goat Jumped in at Once.

THE · FISHERMAN · AND · THE · LITTLE · FISH

A Fisherman cast his net into the sea, and when he drew it up again it contained nothing but a single tiny Fish that begged to be put back into the water.

"I'm only a little fish now," it said, "but I shall grow big one day, and then if you come and catch me again I shall be of more use to you."

But the Fisherman replied, "Oh, no, I shall keep you now I've got you: if I put you back, should I ever see you again? Not likely!"

✳

A bird in the hand is worth two in the bush.

"I'm Only a Little Fish Now."

THE · BOASTING · TRAVELER

A Man once went abroad on his travels, and when he came home he had wonderful tales to tell of the things he had done in foreign countries.

Among other things, he said he had taken part in a jumping-match at Rhodes, and had done a wonderful jump which no one could beat. "Just go to Rhodes and ask them," he said; "every one will tell you it's true."

But one of those who were listening said, "If you can jump as well as all that, we needn't go to Rhodes to prove it. Let's just imagine this is Rhodes for a minute: and now — jump!"

✳

Deeds, not words.

He Had Wonderful Tales to Tell.

THE · CRAB · AND · HIS · MOTHER

An Old Crab said to her son, "Why do you walk sideways like that, my son? You ought to walk straight."

The Young Crab replied, "Show me how, dear mother, and I'll follow your example."

The Old Crab tried, but tried in vain, and then saw how foolish she had been to find fault with her child.

✻

Example is better than precept.

"Why Do You Walk Sideways?"

THE · DONKEY · AND · HIS · SHADOW

A certain man hired a Donkey for a journey in summer time, and started out, the owner following behind to drive the beast.

By and by, in the heat of the day, they stopped to rest, and the traveler wanted to lie down in the Donkey's Shadow; but the owner, who himself wished to be out of the sun, wouldn't let him do that; for he said he had hired out the Donkey only, and not his Shadow. The other maintained that his bargain secured him complete control of the Donkey for the time being.

From words they came to blows; and while they were belaboring each other the Donkey took to his heels and was soon out of sight.

*

*No situation is so bad it can't
be turned to someone's profit.*

From Words They Came to Blows.

THE · FARMER · AND · HIS · SONS

A Farmer, being at death's door, and desiring to impart to his Sons a secret of much importance, called them round him and said, "My Sons, I am shortly about to die; I would have you know, therefore, that in my vineyard there lies a hidden treasure. Dig, and you will find it."

As soon as their father was dead, the Sons took spade and fork and turned up the soil of the vineyard over and over again, in their search for the treasure which they supposed to lie buried there. They found none; however the vines, after so thorough a digging, produced a crop such as had never before been seen.

✳

More treasure than gold can be found beneath the sun.

The Sons Took Spade and Fork.

THE · MONKEY · AS · KING

A t a gathering of all the animals, the Monkey danced and delighted them so much that they made him their King.

The Fox, however, was very much disgusted at the promotion of the Monkey: so having one day found a trap with a piece of meat in it, he took the Monkey there and said to him, "Here is a dainty morsel I have found, sire; I did not take it myself, because I thought it ought to be reserved for you, our King. Will you be pleased to accept it?"

The Monkey made at once for the meat and got caught in the trap. Then he bitterly reproached the Fox for leading him into danger.

But the Fox only laughed and said, "O Monkey, you call yourself King of the Beasts and haven't more sense than to be taken in like that!"

✳

There's more than one way to bait a trap.

The Monkey Danced and Delighted Them.

THE · OLD · LION

A Lion, no longer able to get food by force, determined to do so by cunning.

He lay down inside a cave and pretended to be sick, and when any other animals came to inquire after his health, he sprang upon them and ate them.

Many lost their lives, till one day a Fox came and, suspecting the truth, called the Lion from outside instead of going in.

The Lion said that he was in a very bad way. "But," said he, "why do you stand outside? Pray come in."

"I would do so," answered the Fox, "if I hadn't seen that all the footprints point into the cave but none come out."

※

Your own eyes may be your best witness.

He Pretended to be Sick.

THE · BOY · BATHING

A Boy was bathing in a river and got out of his depth, and was in great danger of being drowned.

A man who was passing along a road close by heard his cries for help, and went to the riverside and began to scold him for being so careless as to get into deep water, but made no attempt to help him.

"Oh, sir," cried the Boy, "please help me first and scold me afterwards!"

✳

Give assistance, not advice, in a crisis.

"Please Help Me First!"

THE · QUACK · FROG

Once upon a time a Frog came forth from his home in the marshes and proclaimed to all the world that he was a learned physician, skilled in drugs and able to cure all diseases.

Among the crowd was a Fox, who called out, "You, a doctor! Why, how can you set up to heal others when you cannot even cure your own lame legs and blotched and wrinkled skin?"

✳

Physician, heal thyself.

"You, a Doctor!"

THE · SWOLLEN · FOX

A hungry Fox found a quantity of bread and meat in a hollow tree, which some shepherds had placed there.

Delighted with his find he slipped in through the narrow opening and greedily devoured it all. But when he tried to get out again, he found himself so swollen after his big meal that he could not squeeze through the hole, and fell to whining and groaning over his misfortune.

Another Fox, happening to pass that way, came and asked him what the matter was; and, on learning the state of the case, said, "Well, my friend, I see nothing for it but for you to stay where you are till you shrink to your former size; you'll get out then easily enough."

✳

Don't get too big for your britches.

He Found Himself So Swollen.

THE · MOUSE · THE · FROG · AND · THE · HAWK

A Mouse and a Frog were friends; they were not really suited, for the Mouse lived entirely on land, while the Frog was at home on land or in water.

So that they might not be separated, the Frog tied them together by the leg with a piece of thread.

On dry land all went well, but, coming to a pool, the Frog jumped in, taking the Mouse with him, and began swimming about.

The unhappy Mouse was drowned, and floated on the surface. He was spied by a Hawk, who pounced down and seized him.

The Frog couldn't loosen the knot binding him to the Mouse, and was carried off and also eaten by the Hawk.

✳

Start wrong, end wrong.

The Frog Tied the Mouse and Himself Together.

THE · BOY · AND · THE · NETTLES

A Boy was gathering berries from a hedge when his hand was stung by a Nettle. Smarting with the pain, he ran to tell his mother, and said to her between his sobs, "I only touched it ever so lightly, mother."

"That's just why you got stung, my son," said she; "if you had grasped it firmly, it wouldn't have hurt you in the least."

✳

Hold strongly to what you want.

He Ran to Tell His Mother.

JUPITER · AND · THE · TORTOISE

Jupiter was about to marry a wife, and determined to celebrate the event by inviting all the animals to a banquet. They all came except the Tortoise, who did not put in an appearance, much to Jupiter's surprise.

So when he next saw the Tortoise he asked him why he had not been at the banquet.

"I don't care for going out," said the Tortoise, "there's no place like home."

Jupiter was so much annoyed by this reply that he decreed that from that time forth the Tortoise should carry his house upon his back, and never be able to get away from home even if he wished to.

✳

It doesn't pay to anger the gods.

They All Came Except the Tortoise.

THE · JACKDAW · AND · THE · PIGEONS

A Jackdaw, watching some Pigeons in a farmyard, envied how well they were fed, and determined to disguise himself as one of them.

He painted himself white and joined the flock; and, so long as he was silent, they never suspected that he was not a pigeon.

But one day he started chattering, and they at once saw through his disguise and pecked him so unmercifully that he was glad to join his own kind again.

But the other Jackdaws did not recognize him in his white dress, and would not let him feed with them, but drove him away: and so he became a homeless wanderer.

✳

To thine ownself, be true.

He Painted Himself White.

THE · PEASANT · AND · THE · APPLE-TREE

A Peasant had an Apple-tree which bore no fruit, but provided a shelter for the sparrows and grasshoppers which chirped in its branches. Disappointed at its barrenness he determined to cut it down, and fetched his ax.

But the sparrows and the grasshoppers begged him to spare it, and said to him, "If you destroy the tree we shall have to seek shelter elsewhere, and you will no longer have our merry chirping to enliven your work in the garden."

He refused to listen and set to work to cut through the trunk. Then he saw that it was hollow and contained a swarm of bees and a large store of honey.

Delighted with his find he threw down his ax, saying, "The old tree is worth keeping after all."

✳

Utility is most men's test of worth.

It was Hollow Inside.

THE · OXEN · AND · THE · AXLE

A pair of Oxen were drawing a heavily loaded wagon along the highway, and, as they tugged and strained at the yoke, the Axles creaked and groaned terribly.

This was too much for the Oxen, who turned round indignantly and said, "You there! Why do you make such a noise when we do all the work?"

✳

They complain most who suffer least.

A Heavily Loaded Wagon.

THE · BOY · AND · THE · FILBERTS

A Boy put his hand into a jar of Filberts, and grasped as many as his fist could possibly hold. But when he tried to pull it out again, he found he couldn't do so, for the neck of the jar was too small to allow for the passage of so large a handful.

Unwilling to lose the nuts but unable to withdraw his hand, he burst into tears.

A bystander, who saw where the trouble lay, said to him, "Come, my Boy, don't be so greedy: be content with half the amount, and you'll be able to get your hand out without difficulty."

✳

Do not attempt too much at once.

The Neck was Too Small.

THE · FOX · WITHOUT · A · TAIL

A Fox once fell into a trap, and after a struggle managed to get free, but with the loss of his tail.

He was then so much ashamed of his appearance that he thought life was not worth living unless he could persuade the other Foxes to part with their tails also, and thus divert attention from his own loss.

So he called a meeting of all the Foxes, and advised them to cut off their tails: "They're ugly things anyhow," he said, "and besides they're heavy, and it's tiresome to be always carrying them about with you."

But one of the other Foxes said, "My friend, if you hadn't lost your own tail, you wouldn't be so keen on getting us to cut off ours."

✳

Beware of those who wish to bring you down, not up.

He Called a Meeting of All the Foxes.

THE · TRAVELER · AND · HIS · DOG

A Traveler was about to start on a journey, and said to his Dog, who was stretching himself by the door, "Come, what are you yawning for? Hurry up and get ready: I mean you to go with me."

But the Dog merely wagged his tail and said quietly, "I'm ready, master: it's you I'm waiting for."

✳

Sometimes the slow ones blame the active for the delay.

The Dog Wagged His Tail.

THE · SHIPWRECKED · MAN · AND · THE · SEA

A shipwrecked Man cast up on the beach fell asleep after his struggle with the waves.

When he woke up, he bitterly reproached the Sea for its treachery in enticing men with its smooth and smiling surface, and then, when they were well embarked, turning in fury upon them and sending both ship and sailors to destruction.

The Sea arose in the form of a woman, and replied, "Lay not the blame on me, O sailor, but on the Winds. By nature I am as calm and safe as the land itself: but the Winds fall upon me with their gusts and gales, and lash me into a fury that is not natural to me."

✳

The blame doesn't always lie with the obvious.

The Sea Arose in the Form of a Woman.

THE · WILD · BOAR · AND · THE · FOX

A wild Boar was engaged in sharpening his tusks on the trunk of a tree in the forest when a Fox came by and, seeing what he was at, said to him, "Why are you doing that, pray? The huntsmen are not out today, and there are no other dangers at hand that I can see."

"True, my friend," replied the Boar, "but the instant my life is in danger, I shall need to use my tusks. There'll be no time to sharpen them then!"

✳

Prepare your defenses before the enemy appears.

Sharpening His Tusks

MERCURY · AND · THE · SCULPTOR

Mercury wanted to know in what estimation he was held by mankind, so he disguised himself as a man and went to a Sculptor's studio, where there were a number of statues.

Seeing a statue of Jupiter, he asked the price.

"A crown," said the Sculptor.

"Is that all?" said he, laughing; and pointing to one of Juno, "how much is that?"

"That," was the reply, "is half a crown."

"And how much for that one over there?" he continued, pointing to a statue of himself.

"Oh, I'll throw him in for nothing if you'll buy the other two," said the Sculptor.

*

Nobody can judge his own worth.

A Number of Statues Ready For Sale

THE · FAWN · AND · HIS · MOTHER

A Hind said to her Fawn, who was now well grown and strong, "My son, Nature has given you a powerful body and a stout pair of horns, and I can't think why you are such a coward as to run away from the hounds."

Just then they both heard the sound of a pack in full cry, but at a considerable distance. "You stay where you are," said the Hind; "never mind me." And with that she ran off as fast as her legs could carry her.

✳

A coward cannot be taught courage.

"Nature Has Given You a Powerful Body."

THE · STAG · AT · THE · POOL

A thirsty Stag went to a Pool to drink. As he saw his own reflection in the water, he was struck with admiration for his fine antlers, but at the same time felt disgust for the weakness and slenderness of his legs.

While he stood there, he was attacked by a Lion; but he drew away from his pursuer, and kept his lead as the ground over which he ran was open and free of trees.

But coming to a wood, he was caught by his antlers in the branches, and fell victim to his enemy.

"Woe is me!" he cried with his last breath, "I despised my legs, which might have saved my life, but gloried in my horns, which have proved my ruin."

✳

What is worth most is often valued least.

He Bent Over the Surface.

THE · DOG · AND · THE · SHADOW

Dog was crossing a plank bridge over a stream with a piece of meat in his mouth, when he happened to see his own reflection in the water.

He thought it was another Dog with a piece of meat twice as big, so he let go his own, and flew at the other Dog to get the larger piece.

But, of course, all that happened was that he got neither: for one was only a Shadow, and the other was carried away by the current.

✳

If you grasp at the shadow, you may lose the substance.

He Flew at the Other Dog.

THE · PEACOCK · AND · JUNO

The Peacock was unhappy because he had not a beautiful voice, and he complained to Juno about it. "The nightingale's song," said he, "is the envy of all the birds; but when I utter a sound I become a laughingstock."

The goddess answered him, saying, "You excel in beauty: your neck flashes like emerald and your tail is of gorgeous color."

But the Peacock was not appeased. "What is the use," said he, "of being beautiful, with a voice like mine?"

Juno replied, "Fate has allotted to all their destined gifts: to you beauty, to the eagle strength, to the nightingale song, and so on; you alone are dissatisfied. Make no more complaints: for, if your present wish *were* granted, you would quickly find cause for fresh discontent."

✳

The farthest you go is with using your own gifts.

"Your Neck Flashes Like Emerald."

THE · EAGLE · AND · THE · ARROW

An Eagle sat perched on a lofty rock, keeping a sharp look-out for prey. A huntsman, concealed in a cleft of the mountain and on the watch for game, spied him there and shot an Arrow at him.

The shaft struck him full in the breast and pierced him through and through. As he lay in the agonies of death, he turned his eyes upon the Arrow.

"Ah! Cruel fate," he cried, "that I should perish thus! But oh! Fate more cruel still, that the Arrow which kills me should be winged with an Eagle's feathers!"

✳

Misfortunes we bring on ourselves are doubly bitter.

Concealed in a Cleft of the Mountain

THE · FARMER · AND THE · VIPER

One winter a Farmer found a Viper frozen and numb with cold, and out of pity picked it up and placed it in his bosom.

The Viper was no sooner revived by the warmth than it turned upon its benefactor and inflicted a fatal bite upon him; and as the poor man lay dying, he cried, "I have only got what I deserved, for taking compassion on so villainous a creature."

✳

Kindness is thrown away upon the evil.

Out of Pity

THE · TWO · FROGS

wo Frogs were neighbors. One lived in a marsh, where there was plenty of water, which frogs love: the other in a lane some distance away, where all the water to be had was that which lay in ruts after the rain.

The marsh Frog warned his friend and pressed him to come and live with him in the marsh, for he would find his quarters there far more comfortable and — what was still more important — more safe.

But the other Frog refused, saying that he could not bring himself to move from a place to which he had become accustomed.

A few days afterwards a heavy wagon came down the lane, and he was crushed to death under the wheels.

✳

There can be great danger in falling in a rut.

There was Plenty of Water

THE · TRAVELERS · AND · THE · PLANE-TREE

Two Travelers were walking along a bare and dusty road in the heat of a summer's day. Coming presently to a Plane-tree, they joyfully turned aside to get shelter from the burning rays of the sun in the deep shade of its spreading branches.

As they rested, looking up into the tree, one of them remarked to his companion, "What a useless tree the Plane is! It bears no fruit and is of no service to man at all."

The Plane-tree interrupted him with indignation. "You ungrateful creature!" it cried. "You come and take shelter under me from the scorching sun, and then, in the very act of enjoying the cool shade of my foliage, you abuse me and call me good for nothing!"

✱

Many a service is met with ingratitude.

"You Ungrateful Creature!"

THE · FLEA · AND · THE · OX

A Flea once said to an Ox, "How comes it that a big strong fellow like you is content to serve mankind, and do all their hard work for them, while I, who am no bigger than you see, live on their bodies and drink my fill of their blood, and never do a stroke for it all?"

To which the Ox replied, "Men are very kind to me, and so I am grateful to them: they feed and house me well, and every now and then they show their fondness for me by patting me on the head and neck."

"They'd pat me, too," said the Flea, "if I let them: but I take good care they don't, or there would be nothing left of me!"

*

One man's pat is another's swat.

"A Big Strong Fellow Like You."

THE · BIRDS · THE · BEASTS · AND · THE · BAT

The Birds were at war with the Beasts, and many battles were fought with varying success on either side. The Bat did not throw in his lot definitely with either party, but when things went well for the Birds he was found fighting in their ranks; when, on the other hand, the Beasts got the upper hand, he was to be found among them.

No one paid any attention to him while the war lasted: but when it was over, and peace was restored, neither the Birds nor the Beasts would have anything to do with so double-faced a traitor, and so he remains to this day a solitary outcast from both.

✳

Don't play both sides against the middle.

He Was Found Fighting in Their Ranks.

THE · MAN · AND · HIS · TWO · SWEETHEARTS

A Man, whose hair was turning grey, had two Sweethearts, an old woman and a young one.

The elder didn't like having him look so much younger than herself; so, whenever he came to see her, she pulled the dark hairs out of his head to make him look old.

The younger didn't like him to look older than herself, and pulled out the grey hairs, to make him look young.

Between them, they left not a hair in his head, and he became perfectly bald.

❋

He who gives in to others' wants
will have no principles of his own.

He Became Perfectly Bald.

THE · WOLF · AND · THE · BOY

A Wolf, who had just enjoyed a good meal and was in a playful mood, caught sight of a Boy lying flat upon the ground, and, realizing that he was trying to hide, and that it was fear of himself that made him do this, he went up to him and said, "Aha, I've found you, you see; but if you can say three things to me, the truth of which cannot be disputed, I will spare your life."

The Boy plucked up courage and thought for a moment, and then he said, "First, it is a pity you saw me; secondly, I was a fool to let myself be seen; and thirdly, we all hate wolves because they are always making unprovoked attacks upon our flocks."

The Wolf replied, "Well, what you say is true enough from your point of view; so you may go."

✳

Even a brute may sometimes listen to reason.

A Wolf Caught Sight of a Boy.

THE · STAG · AND · THE · VINE

A Stag, pursued by huntsmen, concealed himself under cover of a thick Vine. The hunters lost track of him and passed by his hiding-place without being aware that he was anywhere near.

Supposing all danger to be over, he presently began to browse on the leaves of the Vine.

The movement drew the attention of the returning huntsmen, and one of them, supposing some animal to be hidden there, shot an arrow into the foliage.

The unlucky Stag was pierced to the heart, and, as he expired, he said, "I deserve my fate for my treachery in feeding upon the leaves of my protector."

✳

Ingratitude sometimes brings its own punishment.

He Began to Graze on the Leaves.

THE · LAMB · CHASED · BY · A · WOLF

A Wolf was chasing a Lamb, which took refuge in a temple.

The Wolf urged it to come out, and said, "If you don't, the priest is sure to catch you and offer you up in sacrifice on the altar."

To which the Lamb replied, "Thanks, I think I'll stay where I am: I'd rather be sacrificed any day than be eaten up by a Wolf."

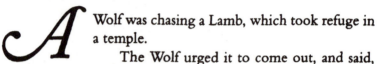

Advice from the greedy is best ignored.

Refuge in a Temple

THE · ARCHER · AND · THE · LION

An Archer went up into the hills to have some sport with his bow, and all the animals fled at the sight of him with the exception of the Lion, who stayed behind and challenged him to fight.

The Archer shot an arrow at the Lion and hit him, and said, "There, you see what my messenger can do: just you wait a moment and I'll tackle you myself."

The Lion, however, when he felt the sting of the arrow, ran away as fast as his legs could carry him.

A Fox, who had seen it all happen, said to the Lion, "Come, don't be a coward: why don't you stay and fight?"

But the Lion replied, "You won't get me to stay, not you: why, when he sends a messenger like that before him, he must himself be terrible to deal with."

✳

Give a wide berth to those who
can do damage at a distance.

The Lion Stayed Behind to Fight.

THE · SICK · STAG

A Stag fell sick and lay in a clearing in the forest, too weak to move from the spot.

When the news of his illness spread, a number of the other beasts came to inquire after his health. They one and all nibbled a little of the grass that grew round the invalid till at last there was not a blade within his reach.

In a few days he began to mend, but was still too feeble to get up and go in search of fodder; and thus he perished miserably of hunger owing to the thoughtlessness of his friends.

✳

Thoughtless friends can be as bad as enemies.

They Nibbled a Little of the Grass.

The · Kingdom · of · the · Lion

*W*hen the Lion reigned over the beasts of the earth he was never cruel or tyrannical, but as gentle and just as a King ought to be.

During his reign he called a general assembly of the beasts, and drew up a code of laws under which all were to live in perfect equality and harmony:

The wolf and the lamb, the tiger and the stag, the leopard and the kid, the dog and the hare, all should dwell side by side in unbroken peace and friendship.

The hare said, "Oh! How I have longed for this day when the weak take their place without fear by the side of the strong!"

✳

Goodness is the greatest strength of all.

The Lion Reigned Over the Beasts.

THE · DONKEY · AND · HIS · DRIVER

A Donkey was being driven down a mountain road, and after jogging along for a while sensibly enough, he suddenly left the track and rushed to the edge of a precipice.

He was just about to leap over the edge when his Driver caught hold of his tail and did his best to pull him back: but pull as he might he couldn't get the Donkey to budge from the brink.

At last the Driver gave up, crying, "All right, then, get to the bottom your own way; but it's the way to sudden death, as you'll find out quick enough."

✳

A willful beast must go his own way.

He Was About to Leap Over the Edge.

THE · LION · AND · THE · HARE

A Lion found a Hare sleeping, and was just going to devour her when he caught sight of a passing stag.

Dropping the Hare, he at once made for the bigger game; but finding, after a long chase, that he could not overtake the stag, he abandoned the attempt and came back for the Hare.

When he reached the spot, however, he found she was nowhere to be seen, and he had to go without his dinner.

"It serves me right," he said; "I should have been content with what I had got, instead of hankering after a better prize."

✳

Be content with what you're sure of.

He Caught Sight of a Passing Stag.

The · Wolves · and · the · Dogs

Once upon a time the Wolves said to the Dogs, "Why should we continue to be enemies? You are very like us in most ways: the difference between us is one of training.

"We live a life of freedom; you are enslaved to men, who beat you, and put collars on you, and compel you to keep watch over their flocks and herds, and give you nothing but bones to eat. Don't put up with it any longer, but hand us over the flocks, and we will all live and feast together."

The Dogs allowed themselves to be persuaded by these words, and accompanied the Wolves into their den. But no sooner were they inside than the Wolves set upon them and tore them to pieces.

✳

Traitors richly deserve their fate.

"Why Should We Be Enemies?"

The · Bull · and · the · Calf

A full-grown Bull was struggling to force his huge bulk through the narrow entrance to a cow-house where his stall was, when a young Calf came up and said to him, "If you'll step aside a moment, I'll show you the way to get through."

The Bull turned upon him with an amused look. "I knew that way," said he, "before you were born."

✳

Respect the wisdom of those who came before you.

"I'll Show You the Way."

THE · TREES · AND · THE · AX

A Woodman went into the forest and begged of the Trees the favor of a handle for his Ax.

The principal Trees at once agreed to so modest a request, and unhesitatingly gave him a young ash sapling, out of which he fashioned the handle he desired.

No sooner had he done so than he set to work to fell the noblest Trees in the wood.

When they saw the use to which he was putting their gift, they cried, "Alas! Alas! We are undone, but we are ourselves to blame. The little we gave has cost us all: had we not sacrificed the rights of the ash, we might ourselves have stood for ages."

✳

*When the rich surrender the rights of the poor,
they endanger their own privileges.*

"We Are Undone!"

THE · ASTRONOMER

There was once an Astronomer whose habit it was to go out at night and observe the stars. One night, as he was walking about outside the town gates, gazing up absorbed into the sky and not looking where he was going, he fell into a dry well.

As he lay there groaning, some one passing by heard him, and, coming to the edge of the well, looked down. On learning what had happened, he said, "If you really were looking so hard at the sky that you didn't even see where your feet were carrying you along the ground, it appears to me that you deserve all you've got."

✳

*You can look at the stars,
but watch where you're going.*

He Fell into a Dry Well.

THE·WORK-DONKEY· AND·THE· WILD·DONKEY

A Wild Donkey, who was wandering idly about, one day came upon a Work-Donkey lying at full length in a sunny spot and thoroughly enjoying himself.

Going up to him, he said, "What a lucky beast you are! Your sleek coat shows how well you live: how I envy you!"

Not long after the Wild Donkey saw his acquaintance again, but this time he was carrying a heavy load, and his driver was following behind and beating him with a thick stick.

"Ah, my friend," said the Wild Donkey, "I don't envy you any more: for I see you pay dear for your comforts."

✳

Advantages that are dearly bought are doubtful blessings.

"What a Lucky Beast You Are!"

THE · ANTS

*A*nts were once men and made their living by tilling the soil.

But, not content with the results of their own work, they were always casting longing eyes upon the crops and fruits of their neighbors, which they stole, whenever they got the chance, and added to their own store.

At last their greediness made Jupiter so angry that he changed them into Ants.

But, though their forms were changed, their nature remained the same: and so, to this day, they go about among the cornfields and gather the fruits of others' labor, and store them up for their own use.

❋

You may punish a thief, but his habits remain.

Jupiter Changed Them into Ants.

THE · FROGS · AND · THE · WELL

Two Frogs lived together in a marsh.

But one hot summer the marsh dried up, and they left it to look for another place to live in: for Frogs like damp places if they can get them.

By and by they came to a deep Well, and one of them looked down into it, and said to the other, "This looks a nice cool place: let us jump in and settle here."

But the other, who had a wiser head on his shoulders, replied, "Not so fast, my friend: supposing this well dried up like the marsh, how should we get out again?"

✳

Think twice before you act.

They Came to a Deep Well.

THE · CRAB ·
AND · THE · FOX

A Crab once left the sea shore and went and settled in a meadow some way inland, which looked very nice and green and seemed likely to be a good place to feed in.

But a hungry Fox came along and spied the Crab and caught him.

Just as he was going to be eaten up, the Crab said, "This is just what I deserve; for I had no business to leave my natural home by the sea and settle here as though I belonged to the land."

✳

Be happy with what you have.

A Hungry Fox Came Along.

THE · FOX · AND · THE · GRASSHOPPER

A Grasshopper sat chirping in the branches of a tree. A Fox heard her, and, thinking what a dainty morsel she would make, he tried to get her down by a trick.

Standing below in full view of her, he praised her song in the most flattering terms, and begged her to descend, saying he would like to make the acquaintance of the owner of so beautiful a voice.

But she was not to be taken in, and replied, "You are very much mistaken, my dear sir, if you imagine I am going to come down: I keep well out of the way of you and your kind ever since the day when I saw numbers of Grasshoppers' wings strewn about the entrance to a Fox's hole."

✳

Flattery should get you nowhere.

A Grasshopper Sat Chirping.

The · Donkey · and · the · Dog

A Donkey and a Dog, traveling together, found a sealed packet on the ground.

The Donkey picked it up, broke the seal, and read it out aloud to the Dog.

It turned out to be all about grass and barley and hay — all the kinds of fodder that Donkeys are fond of.

The Dog was a good deal bored with listening to all this, till at last his impatience got the better of him, and he cried, "Just skip a few pages, friend, and see if there isn't something about meat and bones."

The Donkey glanced through the packet, but found nothing of the sort, and said so.

Then the Dog said in disgust, "Oh, throw it away, what's the good of a thing like that?"

✳

To each his own.

A Donkey and a Dog Traveled Together.

THE · GOATHERD · AND · THE · GOAT

A Goatherd was one day gathering his flock to return to the fold, when one of his Goats strayed and refused to join the rest.

He tried for a long time to get her to return by calling and whistling to her, but the Goat took no notice of him at all; so at last he threw a stone at her and broke one of her horns.

In dismay, he begged her not to tell his master: but she replied, "You silly fellow, my horn would cry aloud even if I held my tongue."

✳

It's no use trying to hide what can't be hidden.

He Threw a Stone at Her.

THE · SHEEP · AND · THE · DOG

A flock of Sheep complained to the shepherd about the difference in his treatment of themselves and his Dog.

"Your conduct," said they, "is very unfair. We provide you with wool and lambs and milk. You give us nothing but grass, and even that we have to find for ourselves: you get nothing at all from the Dog, yet you feed him from your own table."

This was overheard by the Dog, who at once said, "Yes, and quite right, too: where would you be if not for me? Thieves would steal you! Wolves would eat you! If I didn't keep constant watch over you, you would be too terrified even to graze!"

The Sheep acknowledged that he spoke truth, and never again spoke against the regard in which he was held by his master.

✳

The other fellow's plate always looks fuller than our own.

"We Provide You with Wool and Lambs and Milk."

THE · PIG · AND · THE · SHEEP

A Pig found his way into a meadow where a flock of Sheep were grazing.

The shepherd caught him, and was proceeding to carry him off to the butcher's when he set up a loud squealing and struggled to get free.

The Sheep rebuked him for making such a to-do, and said to him, "The shepherd catches us regularly and drags us off just like that, and we don't make any fuss."

"No, I dare say not," replied the Pig, "but my case and yours are altogether different: he only wants you for wool, but me he wants for bacon!"

✳

It's easy to cry "coward" when it's not you in danger.

He Struggled to Get Free.

THE · RIVERS · AND · THE · SEA

O nce upon a time all the Rivers combined to protest against the action of the Sea in making their waters salt.

"When we come to you," said they to the Sea, "we are sweet and drinkable: but when once we have mingled with you, our waters become as briny and unpalatable as your own."

The Sea replied shortly, "Keep away from me and you'll remain sweet."

✷

Some people find fault even with the things that benefit them.

"Our Waters Become Salty."

THE · LION · IN · LOVE

A Lion fell deeply in love with the daughter of a Cottager and wanted to marry her; but her father was unwilling to give her to so fearsome a husband, and yet didn't want to offend the Lion, so he hit upon the following solution.

He went to the Lion and said, "I think you will make a very good husband for my daughter: but I cannot consent to your union unless you let me pull your teeth and clip your nails, for my daughter is terribly afraid of them."

The Lion was so much in love that he readily agreed that this should be done.

When once, however, he was thus disarmed, the Cottager was afraid of him no longer, but drove him away with his club.

✳

Misfortune awaits those who love unwisely.

A Lion Fell Deeply in Love.

THE · BEE-KEEPER

A thief found his way into an apiary when the Bee-keeper was away, and stole all the honey. When the Keeper returned and found the hives empty, he was very much upset and stood staring at them for some time.

Before long the bees came back from gathering honey, and, finding their hives overturned and the Keeper standing by, they made for him with their stings.

At this he fell into a passion and cried, "You ungrateful scoundrels, you let the thief who stole my honey get off scot-free, and then you go and sting me who have always taken such good care of you!"

✳

When you hit back make sure
you have the right man.

He was Very Much Upset.

THE · WOLF · AND · THE · HORSE

A Wolf on his rambles came to a field of oats, but, not being able to eat them, he was passing on his way when a Horse came along.

"Look," said the Wolf, "here's a fine field of oats. For your sake I have left it untouched, and I shall greatly enjoy the sound of your teeth munching the ripe grain."

But the Horse replied, "If Wolves could eat oats, my fine friend, you would hardly have indulged your ears at the cost of your belly."

✳

*There is no virtue in giving to others
what is useless to oneself.*

"Here's a Fine Field of Oats."

THE · FISHERMAN · PIPING

A Fisherman who could play the flute went down one day to the seashore with his nets and his flute; and, taking his stand on a projecting rock, began to play a tune, thinking that the music would bring the fish jumping out of the sea.

He went on playing for some time, but not a fish appeared: so at last he threw down his flute and cast his net into the sea, and made a great haul of fish.

When they were landed and he saw them leaping about on the shore, he cried, "You rascals! You wouldn't dance when I piped: but now I've stopped, you can do nothing else!"

✳

The whole world doesn't dance to our own tune.

Taking His Stand on a Projecting Rock

THE · WEASEL · AND · THE · MAN

A Man once caught a Weasel, which was always sneaking about the house, and was just going to drown it in a tub of water, when it begged hard for its life, and said to him, "Surely you haven't the heart to put me to death? Think how useful I have been in clearing your house of the mice and lizards which used to infest it, and show your gratitude by sparing my life."

"You have not been altogether useless, I grant you," said the Man: "but who killed the fowls? Who stole the meat? No, no! You do much more harm than good, and die you shall."

*

The good you do should always outweigh the bad.

A Man Caught a Weasel.

THE · FISHERMAN

A Fisherman went to a river to fish, and, having laid his nets across the stream, he used a stone and a long cord to beat the water in order to drive the fish into the nets.

A cottager who lived close by came and complained that the Fisherman was disturbing the stream and making the water too muddy to drink.

"I am sorry that this bothers you," replied the Fisherman, "but it is by troubling the waters that I gain my living."

✳

Live and let live.

A Fisherman Went to Fish.

THE · HOUND ·
AND · THE · HARE

A Hound chased a Hare for a long time. Then he came up to her and started first to bite and then lick her.

The poor Hare, not knowing what to make of his actions, said, "If you are a friend, why do you bite me? If an enemy, why caress me?"

※

Better a certain enemy than a doubtful friend.

A Hound Chased a Hare.

THE · ARAB · AND · THE · CAMEL

An Arab loaded his Camel, and then asked him whether he preferred to go up or down hill. "Why do you ask, master?" said the Camel dryly. "Is the level way across the desert shut up?"

✳

*Of what use is it to pretend
there is a choice when there is none?*

An Arab Loaded His Camel.

THE · DONKEY · IN · THE · LION'S · SKIN

A Donkey, finding a Lion's Skin, put it on, and, in pretending to be King of the Beasts, frightened the foolish animals he came across.

Before long he met a fox, and tried to frighten him also.

"If I hear a Lion roar, I am scared," said the fox, "but when he brays, whatever he may wear, I know he's only a donkey."

✳

Clothes do not make the man.

He Pretended to be the King of the Beasts.

THE · CROW · AND · THE · SNAKE

A hungry Crow spied a Snake lying asleep in a sunny spot, and, thinking it dead, picked it up in his claws.

He was carrying it off to a place where he could make a meal of it without being disturbed, when the Snake reared its head and bit him.

It was a poisonous Snake, and the bite was fatal, and the dying Crow said, "What a cruel fate is mine! I thought I had made a lucky find, and it has cost me my life!"

✳

Appearances are very often deceiving.

A Snake Lying Asleep

THE · DOGS · AND · THE · FOX

Some Dogs once found a lion's skin, and were worrying it with their teeth.

Just then a Fox came by and said, "You think yourselves very brave, no doubt; but if that were a live lion you'd find his claws a good deal sharper than your teeth."

✳

It's easy to fight someone who can't fight back.

"If That Were a Live Lion . . ."

THE · ROSE · AND · THE · AMARANTH

A Rose and an Amaranth blossomed side by side in a garden, and the Amaranth said to her neighbor, "How I envy you your beauty and your sweet scent! No wonder you are such a universal favorite."

But the Rose replied with a shade of sadness in her voice, "Ah, my dear friend, I bloom but for a time: my petals soon wither and fall, and then I die. But your flowers never fade, even if they are cut; for they are everlasting."

✳

The flower in the vase smiles,
but it can no longer laugh.

Blossomed Side By Side

THE · CROW · AND · THE · RAVEN

A Crow became very jealous of a Raven, because the latter was regarded by men as a bird of omen which foretold the future, and was accordingly held in great respect by them.

The Crow was very anxious to get the same sort of reputation herself; and, one day, seeing some travelers approaching, she flew on to a branch of a tree at the roadside and cawed as loud as she could.

The travelers were in some dismay at the sound, for they feared it might be a bad omen; till one of them, seeing it was a Crow, said to his companions, "It's all right, my friends, we can go on without fear, for it's only a Crow and that means nothing."

※

*Those who pretend to be something they are not
only make themselves ridiculous.*

She Flew Onto a Tree.

THE · MISER

A Miser melted down all his gold into a single lump, which he buried in a field. Every day he would spend long hours gloating over his treasure.

One of his men noticed his frequent visits to the spot, and one day discovered his secret. He went one night, dug up the gold and stole it.

The next day the Miser visited the place and finding his treasure gone, fell to groaning over his loss. Thus he was seen by a neighbor, who asked him what his trouble was.

The Miser told him and the other replied, "Don't take it so much to heart, my friend; put a brick in the hole, and look at it every day: you won't be any worse off than before, for even when you had your gold it was of no earthly use to you."

✳

Unused riches create no good.

He Spent Long Hours Gloating Over His Treasure.

THE · HORSE · AND · THE · STAG

A Horse used to graze in a meadow which he had all to himself.

But one day a Stag came into the meadow, and said he had as good a right to feed there as the Horse, and moreover chose all the best places for himself.

The Horse, wishing to be revenged upon his unwelcome visitor, went and asked a man if he would help him to turn out the Stag.

"Yes," said the man, "I will, but only if you let me put a bridle in your mouth and mount on your back."

The Horse agreed to this, and the two together very soon turned the Stag out of the pasture: but when that was done, the Horse found to his dismay that in the man he had got a master forever.

✳

Vengeance may be worse than the deed that provoked it.

One Day a Stag Came Into the Meadow.

THE · ANT · AND · THE · DOVE

An Ant stood by a river to quench his thirst, but tumbled in and almost drowned.

A Dove, sitting on a nearby tree, saw the Ant in danger; plucking off a leaf, she dropped it into the water so that the Ant, mounting it, was carried safely to the bank.

A little later a hunter was just about to cast his net over the Dove, when the Ant, seeing the danger, bit the hunter, which made him drop the net, and the Dove flew safely away.

✳

One good turn deserves another.

She Dropped It Into the Water.

THE · OAK · AND · THE · REEDS

An Oak that grew on the bank of a river was uprooted by a severe gale of wind, and thrown across the stream. It fell among some Reeds growing by the water, and said to them, "How is it that you, who are so frail and slender, have managed to weather the storm, whereas I, with all my strength, have been torn up by the roots and hurled into the river?"

"You were stubborn," came the reply, "and fought against the storm, which proved stronger than you: but we bow and yield to every breeze, and thus the gale passed harmlessly over our heads."

✳

It's better by far to bend than to break.

It Fell Among Some Reeds.

THE · BLIND · MAN · AND · THE · CUB

There was once a Blind Man who had so fine a sense of touch that, when any animal was put into his hands, he could tell what it was merely by the feel of it.

One day the Cub of a Wolf was put into his hands, and he was asked what it was.

He felt it for some time, and then said, "Indeed, I am not sure whether it is a Wolf's Cub or a Fox's: but this I know — it would never do to trust it in a sheepfold."

❋

Evil tendencies are early shown.

The Cub of a Wolf was Put Into His Hands.

THE · GNAT · AND · THE · BULL

A Gnat alighted on one of the horns of a Bull, and remained sitting there for a considerable time.

When it had rested sufficiently and was about to fly away, it said to the Bull, "Do you mind if I go now?"

The Bull merely raised his eyes and remarked, without interest, "It's all one to me; I didn't notice when you came, and I shan't know when you go away."

✳

We may often be more important in our own eyes than in the eyes of others.

A Gnat Alighted on the Horn of a Bull.

THE · FIR · TREE · AND · THE · BRAMBLE

A Fir-tree was boasting to a Bramble, and said, somewhat contemptuously, "You poor creature, you are of no use whatever. Now, look at me: I am useful for all sorts of things, particularly when men build houses; they can't do without me then."

But the Bramble replied, "Ah, that's all very well: but you wait till they come with axes and saws to cut you down, and then you'll wish you were a Bramble and not a Fir."

✻

Better poverty without a care
than wealth with its many obligations.

"I Am Useful for All Sorts of Things."

THE · FROGS' · COMPLAINT · AGAINST · THE · SUN

Once upon a time the Sun was about to marry.

The Frogs, in terror, all raised their voices to the skies, and Jupiter, disturbed by the noise, asked them what they were croaking about.

They replied, "The Sun is bad enough even while he is single, drying up our marshes with his heat as he does. But what will become of us if he marries and begets other Suns?"

✳

Nature never disobeys her own laws.

The Frogs Raised Their Voices to the Skies.

THE · CROW · AND · THE · PITCHER

A thirsty Crow found a Pitcher with some water in it, but so little was there that, try as she might, she could not reach it with her beak, and it seemed as though she would die of thirst.

At last she hit upon a clever plan. She began dropping pebbles into the Pitcher, and with each pebble the water rose a little higher until at last it reached the brim, and the knowing bird was able to quench her thirst.

✳

Necessity is the mother of invention.

She Began Dropping Pebbles Into the Pitcher.

THE · BOYS · AND · THE · FROGS

Some mischievous Boys were playing on the edge of a pond, and, catching sight of some Frogs swimming about in the shallow water, they began to amuse themselves by pelting them with stones, and they killed several of them.

At last one of the Frogs put his head out of the water and said, "Oh, stop! Stop! I beg of you: what is sport to you is death to us."

✳

One man's meat is another's poison.

Mischievous Boys at the Pond

THE · PEACOCK · AND · THE · CRANE

A Peacock teased a Crane about the dullness of her plumage. "Look at my brilliant colors," said she, "and see how much finer they are than your poor feathers."

"I am not denying," replied the Crane, "that yours are far brighter than mine; but when it comes to flying I can soar into the clouds, whereas you are confined to the earth like any plain chicken."

✳

Looks aren't everything.

"Look at My Brilliant Colors."

THE · OXEN · AND · THE · BUTCHERS

Once upon a time the Oxen determined to be revenged on the Butchers for the destruction they caused in their ranks, and plotted to put them to death.

They were all gathered together discussing how best to carry out the plan, and the more violent of them were engaged in sharpening their horns for the fray, when an old Ox got up upon his feet and said:

"My brothers, you have good reason to hate these Butchers, but, at any rate, they understand their work and do what they have to do without causing us unnecessary pain. But if we kill them, others, who have no experience, will be sent to slaughter us, and will, by their bungling, inflict great sufferings upon us. For you may be sure that, even though all the Butchers perish, mankind will never go without beef."

✳

The enemy you know is better than the enemy you don't.

They Were All Gathered Together.

THE · WOLF · AND · THE · LION

A Wolf stole a lamb from the flock, and was carrying it off to devour it at his leisure when he met a Lion, who took his prey away from him and walked off with it.

The Wolf dared not resist, but when the Lion had gone some distance he said, "It is most unjust of you to take what's mine away from me like that."

The Lion laughed and called out in reply, "It was justly yours, no doubt! The gift of a friend, perhaps?"

✳

Those who live by thievery can't complain of robbers.

"It is Most Unjust of You."

THE · TORTOISE · AND · THE · EAGLE

A Tortoise, discontented with his lowly life, and envious of the birds he saw disporting themselves in the air, begged an Eagle to teach him to fly.

The Eagle protested that it was idle for him to try, as nature had not provided him with wings; but the Tortoise pressed him with entreaties and promises of treasure, insisting that it could only be a question of learning the tricks of the air.

At length the Eagle consented to do the best he could for him, and picked him up in his talons. Soaring with him to a great height in the sky, he then let him go, and the wretched Tortoise fell headlong and was dashed to pieces on a rock.

✳

It's better to keep both your feet on the ground.

The Tortoise Begged the Eagle to Teach Him.

THE · GOAT · ON · THE · HOUSETOP

A Goat climbed up on to the roof of a cottage, attracted by the grass that grew in the thatch; and as he stood there browsing, he caught sight of a Wolf passing below, and jeered at him because he couldn't reach him.

The Wolf only looked up and said, "I hear you, my young friend; but it is not you who mock me, but the height of the roof on which you are standing."

✳

Position is everything in life.

He Caught Sight of a Wolf.

THE · WALNUT · TREE

A Walnut Tree, which grew by the roadside, bore every year a plentiful crop of nuts. Every one who passed by pelted its branches with sticks and stones, in order to bring down the nuts, and the tree suffered severely.

"It is hard," it cried, "that the very persons who enjoy my crop should thus reward me with insults and blows."

✳

Be most kind to those who are most giving.

A Plentiful Crop

THE · MAN · AND · THE · LION

A Man and a Lion were companions on a journey, and in the course of conversation they began to boast about their prowess, and each claimed to be superior to the other in strength and courage. They were still arguing with some heat when they came to a crossroad where there was a statue of a Man strangling a Lion.

"There!" said the Man triumphantly. "Look at that! Doesn't that prove to you that we are stronger than you?"

"Not so fast, my friend," said the Lion: "that is only your view of the case. If we Lions could make statues, you may be sure that in most of them you would see the Man underneath."

✳

There are two sides to every question.

A Man and a Lion Were Companions.

THE · OLIVE-TREE · AND · THE · FIG-TREE

*A*n Olive-tree taunted a Fig-tree with the loss of her leaves at a certain season of the year. "You," she said, "lose your leaves every autumn, and are bare till the spring: whereas I, as you see, remain green and flourishing all the year round."

Soon afterwards there came a heavy fall of snow, which settled on the leaves of the Olive-tree so that she bent and broke under the weight; but the flakes fell harmlessly through the bare branches of the Fig-tree, which survived to bear many more crops.

✳

To everything there is a season, and a purpose.

"I Remain Green All Year."

THE · LION · AND · THE · BOAR

One hot and thirsty day in the height of summer a Lion and a Boar came to a little stream at the very same moment. In a trice they were quarreling as to who should drink first. The quarrel soon became a fight and they attacked one another with utmost fury. Presently, stopping for a moment to take a breath, they saw some vultures seated on a rock above, evidently waiting for one of them to be killed, when they would fly down and feed upon the remains.

The sight sobered them at once, and they made up their quarrel, saying, "We had much better be friends than fight and be eaten by vultures."

✳

Friendship is a hedge against adversity.

A Lion and a Boar Came to a Stream.

THE · FROGS · ASKING · FOR · A · KING

The Frogs were discontented because no one ruled over them, so they asked Jupiter for a King.

Jupiter, despising their folly, cast a log into their pool, and said that would be their King.

The Frogs were terrified by the splash, and jumped to the deepest parts of the pool; but when they saw the log remain motionless, they began to feel such contempt for it that they even took to sitting upon it.

Thinking that King was an insult to their dignity, they sent to Jupiter again, and begged him to take away the sluggish King and to give them another and a better one.

Jupiter sent a Stork to rule them, who arrived and began to catch and eat the Frogs as fast as he could.

✳

That governs best which governs least.

The Frogs Were Terrified by the Splash.

*F*ATHER · AND · *S*ONS

A Man had several Sons who were always quarreling with one another, and, try as he might, he could not get them to live together in harmony. So he determined to convince them of their folly by the following means. Bidding them fetch a bundle of sticks, he invited each in turn to break it across his knee.

All tried and all failed: and then he undid the bundle, and handed them the sticks one by one, which they had no difficulty at all in breaking.

"There, my boys," said he, "united you will be more than a match for your enemies: but if you quarrel and separate, your weakness will put you at the mercy of those who attack you."

✳

In union is strength.

He Handed Them the Sticks One by One.

THE · LAMP

A Lamp, well filled with oil, burned with a clear and steady light, and began to swell with pride and boast that it shone more brightly than the sun himself. Just then a puff of wind came and blew it out.

Someone struck a match and lit it again, and said, "You just keep alight, and never mind the sun. Nor do the stars ever need to be relit as you had to be just now."

❋

Our own vanity is the worst flatterer.

The Lamp Swelled with Pride.

THE · HAWK · THE · FROG · AND · THE · MOUSE

A Frog and a Mouse fought about who should rule the swamp they lived in.

The clever Mouse, hidden under the grass, made sudden attacks on the frog, taking him at a disadvantage. The Frog was stronger than the Mouse though, and to end the dispute, challenged the Mouse to a duel.

The Mouse accepted; each came armed with the sharp point of a reed, each sure of his own success.

A Hawk was flying above and saw the little animals so intent on fighting. She swooped down, seized them both in her strong talons, and carried them off to feed her young.

✳

People who fight give opportunities to their enemies.

A Frog and a Mouse Fought.

THE · MICE · IN · COUNCIL

A number of Mice once had a meeting to decide the best means of ridding their community of a Cat that had killed many of their companions. Several plans were brought forth and rejected. At last, a young Mouse suggested that a bell be hung round the tyrant's neck, that they might be warned of her coming and be able to escape.

Everyone loved the idea, except one old Mouse, who was silent for some time, but then got up and said, "The plan is very clever, and would be successful if carried out. I would like to know *who* is going to bell the cat."

✳

It is easier to make a suggestion than to carry it out.

The Mice Had a Meeting.

THE · MULE

A Mule began one day to jump and run about, until she was completely convinced that she could outrun any animal at any speed.

"My mother was a race-horse," she thought, "and I can run just as fast!"

But running had such an effect on her, that she became thoroughly exhausted.

It was then that she remembered that her father was only a donkey.

✳

There are two sides to every truth.

"And I Can Run Just As Fast!"

THE · BAT · AND · THE · WEASELS

A Bat fell to the ground and was captured by a Weasel. The Bat begged the Weasel not to kill him.

"Alas," said the Weasel, "I cannot free you, for the Weasel is the enemy of all birds."

"But I'm not a bird, I'm a mouse!" exclaimed the Bat.

"I see you are," said the Weasel, "now that I look closely at you," and he let him go.

Sometime after the Bat was caught by another Weasel, and once more he found himself pleading for his life.

"No," said this Weasel, "I have never ever let a mouse free."

"But I'm not a mouse," said the Bat, "I'm a bird."

"Why, yes you are," replied the Weasel, and he let the Bat go.

✳

See how the wind blows before making a commitment.

A Bat Fell to the Ground.

THE · BEAR · AND · THE · FOX

A Bear was boasting one day of his great love for mankind, saying that he had such a respect for humans that he would not even touch a dead body.

A Fox nearby said smiling, "I would think more of your love if you never ate them alive."

✳

Kindness is better given to the living than to the dead.

"I Would Think More of Your Love."

THE · WOLF · AND · THE · GOAT

A Wolf saw a young Goat, who was feeding at the top of a high cliff where the Wolf could not reach him. He called up to the Goat: "Be careful or you may fall. If you come down here, the grass is much sweeter, and you'll find much more of it."

"Thank you," said the little Goat, "but I like it very much here. If I came down to you, it is you who would feed better, not I."

✳

The advice of an enemy is not to be trusted.

A Young Goat, Feeding on Top of a Cliff

THE · DOG · IN · THE · MANGER

A Dog once made his bed in a Manger, where he lay nipping and growling, keeping the Horses from getting their food.

"What a mean animal that one is!" said a Horse. "He cannot eat the corn himself and he won't let us eat it who are hungry."

✳

Live and let live.

A Dog Made His Bed in a Manger

THE · DOG · AND · THE · WOLF

A Dog was asleep in the sun in a farmyard when a Wolf pounced on him.

Pleading for his life, the Dog said, "Please Wolf, see how thin I am and what a poor meal I would be now. If you will wait a few days, my master is giving a feast. All the rich scraps and pickings will be mine. I shall be full and fat and then will be a good time for you to eat me."

The Wolf thought this made sense, and he left. Some time afterward he came back to the farm, and there was the Dog, out of his reach on the stable roof. "Come down," the Wolf called, "don't you remember our agreement?"

But the Dog said, "My dear friend, if you ever catch me on the ground again, don't wait for any feast."

✳

Once bitten, twice shy.

Pleading for His Life

THE · VAIN · JACKDAW

A Jackdaw, as conceited as a Jackdaw can be, picked up some peacock feathers which the original owners had shed, stuck them among his own, and, ignoring his old friends, went among a flock of the more beautiful Peacocks.

The Peacocks immediately attacked the foolish Jackdaw, ripped off his borrowed feathers, and drove him away with sharp pecks from their beaks.

The unlucky Jackdaw, saddened, went back to his old friends as if he had never left.

But, remembering how he had behaved, the other Jackdaws no longer wanted him as a friend. One of them said:

"If you had been happy with how nature made you, you would not have been attacked by your betters and despised by your equals."

✳

Fine feathers do not make fine birds.

The Jackdaw Stuck the Feathers Among His Own.

THE · GOOSE · THAT · LAID · THE · GOLDEN · EGGS

A Man and his Wife had the good fortune to possess a Goose which laid a Golden Egg every day. Lucky though they were, they began to think they were not getting rich fast enough, and they decided to kill it in order to get all the gold at once.

But when they cut it open, it was just like any other Goose. Thus, they neither got rich all at once, as they had hoped, nor enjoyed any more the daily addition to their wealth.

✳

Much wants more and loses all.

A Golden Egg Every Day